I SPY

WITH MY LITTLE EYE

VALENTINES DAY

Let's Play I SPY

The Letters are not in order, just like a real game of I spy

Little Learners PUBLISHING

I SPY WITH MY LITTLE EYE something beginning with...

E

E LEPHANT!

I SPY WITH MY LITTLE EYE
something beginning with...

Giraffe!

I SPY WITH MY LITTLE EYE
something Beginning with...

P

Pizza!

I SPY WITH MY LITTLE EYE

something beginning with...

Monkey!

I SPY WITH MY LITTLE EYE
something Beginning with...

O

Owl!

BEE!

I SPY WITH MY LITTLE EYE something Beginning with...

F

Fox!

I SPY WITH MY LITTLE EYE
something beginning with...

R

Rabbit!

I SPY WITH MY LITTLE EYE something Beginning with...

Coffee!

I SPY WITH MY LITTLE EYE something beginning with...

H

HEART!

I SPY WITH MY LITTLE EYE something beginning with...

Z

ZEBRA!

I SPY WITH MY LITTLE EYE
something beginning with...

S

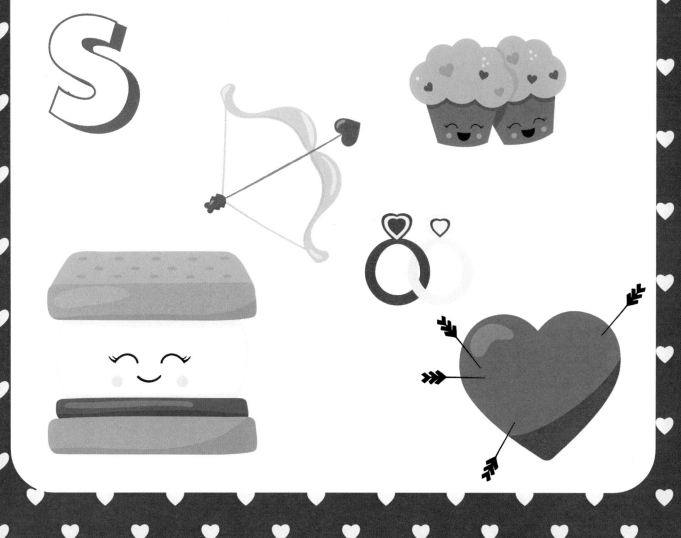

S'MORES!

I SPY WITH MY LITTLE EYE
something Beginning with...

A

I SPY WITH MY LITTLE EYE

something beginning with...

B

BICYCLE!

I SPY WITH MY LITTLE EYE

something Beginning with...

ICE CREAM!

I SPY WITH MY LITTLE EYE
something beginning with...

T

TIGER!

I SPY WITH MY LITTLE EYE something Beginning With...

D

DINOSAUR!

LION!

I SPY WITH MY LITTLE EYE
something Beginning with...

J

JAM!

GREAT JOB PLAYING
I SPY
WITH MY LITTLE EYE
VALENTINES DAY

Made in the USA
Las Vegas, NV
03 February 2021